Judaism's
Great Debates

RABBI BARRY L. SCHWARTZ
AND RABBI MARK H. LEVINE

Judaism's Great Debates
Rabbi Barry L. Schwartz
Rabbi Mark H. Levine

Illustrated By:
John Klossner and David Ricceri

BEHRMAN HOUSE

Behrman House Publishers
11 Edison Place, Springfield, NJ 07081
www.behrmanhouse.com
www.behrmanhouse.com/greatdebates

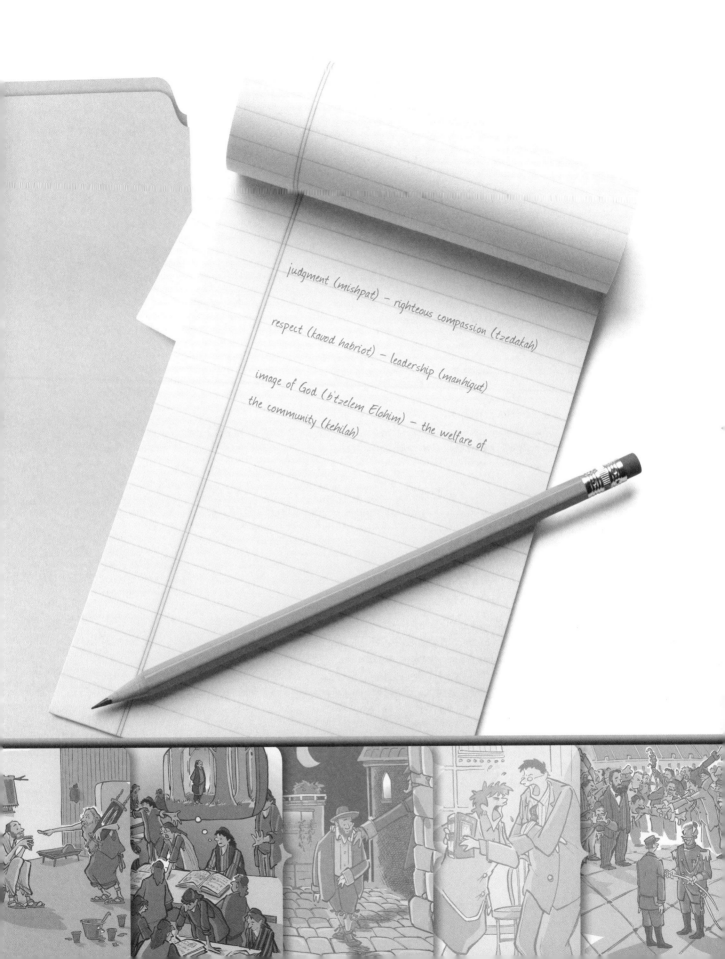

judgment (mishpat) — righteous compassion (tzedakah)

respect (kavod habriot) — leadership (manhigut)

image of God (b'tzelem Elohim) — the welfare of
the community (kehilah)

Design:

Linda V. Curran

Special thanks to Avi S. West and Lisa Micley who read and commented on portions of the text.

Copyright © Behrman House, Inc.
Published by Behrman House, Inc.
Springfield, NJ 07081
www.behrmanhouse.com
Visit www.behrmanhouse.com/greatdebates

ISBN 978-0-87441-852-1
Manufactured in the United States of America
Library of Congress Control Number: 2012001783

With special thanks to David Behrman and David Lerman, this book is dedicated to my students and to all young debaters. —B. Schwartz

With enduring love, I dedicate this book to my wife and dearest friend, Lisa Horowitz. —M. Levine

---

Photography Credits
Page 7—"Beit haMidrash"—Shoshannah Brombacher, Ph.D.
Page 17—Eastern State Penitentiary—Tom Bernard
Page 23—Girl thinking—Ant Clausen
Page 29—Ruth Bader Ginsburg—Steve Petteway, Collection of the Supreme Court of the United States
Page 35—United States Supreme Court—Gary Blakeley
Page 41—Boy thinking—ATurner
Page 47—Entrance of the Cave of Coffins, in the Bet Shearim National Park (Israel)
Page 53—Rabbi Adin Steinsaltz—Erik Tisch
Page 59—Girl thinking—Karina Bakalyan
Page 65—Rabbi Sara Hurwitz—Erika deVries
Page 71—Supreme Court of Israel—Corky Buczyk

CONTENTS

Introduction **6**

CHAPTER **1** **Abraham & God** **12**

CHAPTER **2** Moses & Korach 18

CHAPTER **3** **The Five Daughters & the Twelve Tribes** 24

CHAPTER **4** **David & Nathan** **30**

CHAPTER **5** Ben Zakkai & the Zealots 36

CHAPTER **6** **Hillel & Shammai** **42**

CHAPTER **7** **The Vilna Gaon & the Ba'al Shem Tov** **48**

CHAPTER **8** Spinoza & the Amsterdam Rabbis 54

CHAPTER **9** Geiger, Hirsch & Frankel 60

CHAPTER **10** Herzl & Wise **66**

Online Resources 70

Introduction

One of the most extraordinary legends in the Talmud describes a heated argument between Rabbi Eliezer ben Hyrcanus and his colleagues about the ritual purity of an oven. Don't be fooled by the obscure topic; this tale sparkles with eye-popping special effects and a surprise ending.

It has been taught: On the day of the debate, Rabbi Eliezer brought forward every imaginable argument that the oven was ritually clean. The sages, however, refused to accept them.

Rabbi Eliezer said to them: "If the law agrees with me, let this carob tree prove it!" Whereupon the carob tree was torn 100 cubits out of its place — others say 400 cubits out of its place.

"No proof can be brought from a carob tree," the sages replied.

Again Rabbi Eliezer said to them: "If the law agrees with me, let this stream of water prove it!" Whereupon the stream of water started flowing backwards.

"No proof can be brought from a stream of water," the sages replied.

Again Rabbi Eliezer said to them: "If the law agrees with me, let the walls of this schoolhouse prove it!" Whereupon the walls of the schoolhouse leaned inward, perilously close to collapsing.

But Rabbi Joshua rebuked the walls saying: "When scholars are engaged in a debate of Jewish law, what right have you to interfere?" So the walls did not fall, in honor of Rabbi Joshua, nor did they resume their upright position, in honor of Rabbi Eliezer.

Again Rabbi Eliezer said to them: "If the law agrees with me, let it be proved from Heaven!" Whereupon a voice from Heaven cried out: "Why do you debate with Rabbi Eliezer, seeing that the law agrees with him every time?"

Rabbi Joshua then arose and exclaimed: "The answer is not from Heaven!"

What did the Holy One, blessed be God, do in that hour [after the debate]? God laughed with joy and replied, "My children have defeated Me, My children have defeated Me!"

(Talmud Baba Matzia 59b)

This legend celebrates our right to think for ourselves, to argue fiercely for our point of view, and to interpret the laws of the Torah. Rabbi Joshua's defiant claim that even God lacks authority to overturn the majority's decision enshrines the practice of debate and the principle of majority rule in Jewish culture.

The Spirit of Jewish Debate

The Talmud is the central pillar of Jewish law and behavior. It records hundreds of years of argumentation and debate. Within its pages, rabbis argued with each other not only about the correct way to observe the Torah's commandments, but also about spirituality and philosophy. Because every aspect of Jewish living depended on the outcomes of these debates, the stakes were high and the arguments passionate. And yet, the intellectual adversaries in the Talmud remained polite to each other. Their respectful behavior illustrated a principle first described in *Pirkei Avot* as *machloket l'shem shamayim*, engaging in an argument for the sake of Heaven.

"Every argument that is for the sake of Heaven will make a lasting contribution. Every argument that is not for the sake of Heaven will not make a lasting contribution" (*Pirkei Avot* 5:20).

Debate for the Sake of Heaven

Advocates who argue *l'shem shamayim*, for the sake of Heaven, pursue truth and the community's welfare rather than their own glorification. They never demonize their rivals or attack them personally. On the contrary, they respect their adversaries as human beings and acknowledge the merits of their opinions. As an example of debate *l'shem shamayim*, the Talmud depicts confrontations between the schools of Hillel and Shammai for dominance in the Great Sanhedrin—the highest court in ancient Israel.

Hillel's followers—Beit Hillel—argued that the law should be decided in accordance with their views, while Shammai's followers—Beit Shammai—claimed the law should be interpreted according to their methods.

"*Then a voice from Heaven announced: 'Both are the words of the living God… but the law is in agreement with the ruling of Beit Hillel.'*"

An anonymous questioner wonders, "*Since both are the words of the living God, what was it that entitled the school of Hillel to have the law fixed in agreement with its rulings?*"

The Talmud answers: "*Because it [Beit Hillel] was kindly and modest, it studied its own rulings and those of the school of Shammai, and was even so [humble] as to mention the actions of the school of Shammai before its own.*"

Respect for differences of opinion led the compilers of the Talmud to include minority opinions in the text, a practice adopted centuries later by the United States Supreme Court.

Debate Is the Lifeblood of Judaism

Argumentation and debate is the lifeblood of Judaism. Abraham, the first Jew, challenged God's decision to destroy the innocent along with the guilty in Sodom and Gomorrah. Jacob successfully wrestled with an agent of God and earned a new name, *Israel* (God wrestler), because he "wrestled with God and with men and prevailed" (Genesis 32:29). Moses, like the patriarchs before him, frequently argued with God on the congregation's behalf. With role models like these, it is only natural that Jews throughout history have confronted authority and spoken out on behalf of those who can't speak for themselves. And now, as Jacob's most recent descendents, you have the responsibility to wrestle with the social issues of our times. This book will prepare you for the challenge.

How to Use this Book

In the following chapters, you will read ten great debates in Jewish history. To fully understand the arguments, you must familiarize yourself with the historic context of the disputes. The opening illustration and its accompanying vignette, the history timeline, and the clarification questions in each chapter provide this crucial background information.

Next, read the "Great Debate." It brings alive the voices of the past by mixing fictional dialog with historic sources (which appear in italics), such as the Tanach, Midrash, letters and books written by the debaters, communal archives, and eyewitness accounts.

At the heart of each debate is a values conflict. Values are principles, beliefs, or behaviors that we cherish; for example, honoring one's privacy. In the course of our personal lives, occasions will inevitably arise when values we hold dear will conflict. Imagine the following situation: Two friends tell you a secret and ask you to respect their privacy. The secret, however, involves behaviors that put your friends at risk. Suddenly, you are confronted with a values conflict. If you respect your friends' privacy, they might hurt themselves. If you tell someone about their dangerous behavior, you risk breaking the bonds of friendship. Both values— privacy and friendship—are important, but you must choose one over the other.

Training yourself to understand the "Competing Values" section will prepare you to find similar conflicts in our society; after all, the dilemmas encountered and debated by our ancestors—how to govern, how to decide what is right, and how to understand God and religion—confront us today.

The "Debate It" section in each chapter gives you the opportunity to wrestle with these contemporary challenges. You will find a brief description of a modern issue that shares the same values conflict as the great debate. A resolution is also provided. "Resolution" is a debate term for a topic of discussion that is centered on a values conflict. According to common practice, resolutions are stated as if one side of the dilemma is correct. Here is an example:

RESOLVED: that the protection of public safety justifies random, mandatory personal searches at all public facilities.

During the debate, the affirmative side argues that the resolution is correct, and the negative side argues that it is incorrect.

In values-oriented debates—called Lincoln-Douglas debates—the arguments remain focused on the underlying values conflict. In the sample resolution above, the values conflict is between personal privacy and public security. The affirmative side must argue that national security is more important to society and offer evidence supporting that choice. The negative team must rebut the affirmative claim and state why the ideal of personal privacy is more important to society.

Go and Debate

Judaism has a rich tradition of study, argumentation, and debate. In fact, society associates Jews so closely with debating that a stereotype has developed on the topic. You might have heard the humorous description, "two Jews, three opinions!"

Even more insightful is the following adaptation of a popular joke:
When I first met my best friend, who was not Jewish, we enjoyed long, involved conversations. At least that's what I thought, until my friend complained, 'Why are you always arguing with me?' 'I'm not arguing with you,' I said, 'I'm Jewish.'

As you will discover in this book, Jews do not argue simply to be stubborn. On the contrary, our tradition prizes *machloket l'shem shamayim*, vigorous but respectful debate that advances communal well-being and the pursuit of truth and justice in the world.

CHAPTER **1** Abraham & God

1813 B.C.E.

Abram born

Abram answers God's call to leave his native land and his father's house. He travels to Canaan with Sarai.

Abram and Lot divide the land. Lot settles in Sodom, in the plains of the Jordan River. Abram remains in Canaan

Where's Your Conscience?

> " Will You sweep away the innocent along with the guilty? Shall not the Judge of all the earth deal justly? "
>
> (Abraham, Genesis 18:22, 25)

Imagine a city where people faced the death penalty for giving money to the poor. Or, consider a town where the judges are named Liar, Awful Liar, Forger, and Perverter of Justice. Would you want to live in a wicked place like that? According to rabbinic tradition, life in Sodom and Gomorrah fit this description. Not surprisingly, God decided to destroy these twin cities and rid the world of their evil. Before destroying Sodom, though, the Creator considered telling Abraham what was about to happen.

"Shall I hide from Abraham what I am about to do…?" the Almighty wondered. After all, *"I have singled him out, that he may instruct his children…to keep the way of God by doing what is just and right…"* (Genesis 18:17–19).

When Abraham heard God's plan to destroy the cities, he worried that many innocent people would die along with the guilty citizens of Sodom and Gomorrah. God's solution didn't seem just. In a heroic act of conscience, Abraham confronted God.

1713 B.C.E.

God makes a Covenant with Abram, changes his name to Abraham, and promises him a son.

Abraham circumcises himself, Ishmael, and every male in his household. Messengers of God arrive to comfort him and tell of Isaac's birth.

Messengers of God leave Abraham and go to Sodom. God reveals the plan to destroy Sodom.

Clarification

1 **Why do you think God told Abraham about the plan to destroy Sodom and Gomorrah?** _____

_____

_____

_____

2 **What gave Abraham the courage to confront God?**

_____

_____

_____

3 Punishing the innocent along with the guilty is known as collective punishment. **Can you describe an incident, real or imagined, when collective punishment might be appropriate?**

_____

_____

_____

_____

4 Contrast Noah's behavior when he learned about God's plan to destroy the world (Genesis 6:13–7:5) with Abraham's reaction when God told him about the destruction of Sodom and Gomorrah.

_____

_____

_____

_____

_____

The Great Debate

Based upon Genesis 18:22–32

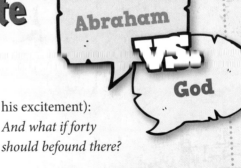
Abraham VS. God

Abraham (tentative at first but with stronger passion as he continues): *Will You sweep away the innocent along with the guilty? What if there should be fifty innocent within the city: Will You then wipe out the place and not forgive it for the sake of the innocent fifty who are in it? Far be it from You to do such a thing, to bring death upon the innocent as well as the guilty, so that innocent and guilty fare alike. Far be it from You! Shall not the Judge of all the earth deal justly?*

God: *If I find within the city of Sodom fifty innocent ones, I will forgive the whole place for their sake.*

Abraham (realizing that God has given him an opening, Abraham seizes the opportunity): Allow me to speak freely, my God, *I who am but dust and ashes: What if the fifty innocent should lack five? Will you destroy the whole city for want of the five?*

God: *I will not destroy it if I find forty-five good people there.*

Abraham (barely able to contain his excitement): *And what if forty should be found there?*

God: For the sake of the forty righteous people, *I will not do it.*

Abraham (wondering if he can press the point further, he continues respectfully): Don't be angry with me, God, if I proceed with this argument: *What if thirty should be found there?*

God: *I will not do it if I find thirty there.*

Abraham (smiling at his apparent success): *I venture again to speak to my God: What if twenty should be found there?*

God: *I will not destroy Sodom, for the sake of those twenty.*

Abraham (triumphantly): Permit me to speak this last time: *What if ten righteous people should be found there?*

God: *I will not destroy, for the sake of the ten.*

15

Cross Examination

Abraham begins the debate with a plea for justice, saying to God, "Will you sweep away the innocent along with the guilty?" **What makes this question a plea for justice?**

_____

_____

_____

Abraham's second question is different. He raises the idea that if fifty righteous people can be found, then the entire population, good and evil, should be spared. **What value is Abraham now demanding from God?**

_____

Do you agree that the merit of a few righteous people can/should outweigh the evil of a majority? _____

_____

Debate It

Our justice system relies heavily on punishment to change criminal behavior. Monetary fines, forced community service, supervised probation, and prison sentences are examples of retributive [ri trib´ yoo tiv] justice, which penalizes offenders in proportion to the pain they have caused victims. "Let the penalty fit the crime" expresses the ideal of retributive justice.

Certain critics of this system argue that retributive justice has failed. They advocate restorative [ri stor´ a tiv] practices, which focus on restoring relationships rather than punishment. Mediation and conferencing with victims and offenders are examples of restorative practices.

Resolved: that the U.S. criminal justice system should be based on restorative practices (righteous compassion) instead of retributive punishments (judgment).

Competing Values

Judgment, מִשְׁפָּט (*mishpat*), must be balanced by righteous compassion, צְדָקָה (*tzedakah*).

Democracy demands that judges and juries ignore their emotions and consider only the facts, but a judicial system without benevolence crushes the human spirit.

Reflections

Abraham's behavior makes him the model of "the just and the right." The Torah says these qualities will characterize Abraham's descendents. (See Genesis 18:19.)

What prevents you from being more compassionate in your behavior toward others? From demanding judgment from others?

Whom do you admire for being compassionate?

What steps can you take today to balance judgment and compassion in the world?

Echoes from the Past

Alfred Fleisher (1878-1928)

hen a new inmate arrived at Eastern State Penitentiary (ESP) in Philadelphia, Pennsylvania, prison guards pulled a hood over the convict's head and led him down a long, stone corridor to an 8-by-12-foot solitary cell. "No prisoner is seen by another after he enters the wall," boasted a warden in 1831. For the remainder of their sentences, condemned prisoners languished in solitary confinement, deprived of contact not only with fellow inmates, but also with the outside world—including their families. Charles Dickens, the famous British author, visited ESP and compared imprisonment there to death. He described the hated hood that newcomers don as a "dark shroud, an emblem of the curtain dropped between [the prisoner] and the living world."

The curtain between humane treatment and cruel solitude lifted in 1913, when solitary confinement at ESP officially ended. Within ten years, programs that prepared inmates for life outside ESP's bleak stone walls were implemented. Prisoners studied together in classrooms, exercised together on ball fields, and prayed together in a chapel. At the center of this reform movement stood Alfred Fleisher, who became president of the prison's board of trustees in 1924. Fleisher, a Jew, also supervised the construction of a small prison synagogue, which he regularly attended. Friends described Fleisher as a caring man, someone with a boundless ability to comprehend human suffering.

1280 B.C.E.

Exodus from Egypt

First rebellion
The community complains
about lack of meat.

During the next forty years, the community
wanders in the wilderness and repeatedly
rebels against Moses' authority.

Second rebellion
Miriam and Aaron complain again
Moses' wife and his authority.

Who's the Boss?

> ❝ For all the community are holy, every one of them, and God is in their midst. Why then do you raise yourselves above God's congregation?
>
> (Korach to Moses, Numbers 16:3) ❞

The hope that filled the Israelites' hearts after they escaped from Egyptian slavery gradually evaporated in the wilderness. Similarly, their trust in God disappeared. Even life-sustaining manna, which the Holy One provided daily, could not keep the ungrateful community from whining, "If only we had meat to eat! Indeed, we were better off in Egypt." (Numbers 11:18). Incensed by their greed, God struck the congregation with a deadly plague at a place called *Kivrot Hata'ava* (the graves of lust), because there, the Children of Israel buried those who could not control their cravings.

And still the murmuring continued. Before entering the Promised Land, Moses sent twelve spies to scout the territory. When they returned, a majority reported that the land was inhabited by giants. Frightened, the people blamed Moses for their plight and plotted against him. God's anger flared again, but Moses pleaded on their behalf. Although the wilderness generation was spared instant death, they were condemned to wander until they died.

On the heels of this rebellion, Korach, Moses' cousin, challenged Moses' spiritual and political leadership.

1240 B.C.E.

Third rebellion
The community complains about the difficulty of conquering the Land of Israel.

Fourth rebellion
Korach and his followers rebel against Moses' authority and Aaron's status as High Priest.

Fifth rebellion
The community complains about lack of water.

Clarification

1 **What leadership traits were required to lead the Children of Israel during their wandering in the wilderness?**

_____

_____

_____

2 **How would you characterize Moses' reaction to each of the rebellions he faced in the wilderness?** _____

_____

_____

_____

3 When the Almighty chose Moses at the burning bush to lead the Jewish people (Exodus 3:1–10), he refused. **Why? What can we learn about leadership from that incident?** _____

_____

_____

_____

_____

4 **If Moses had been a more effective leader, do you think the people would have continuously rebelled?** _____

_____

_____

_____

The Great Debate

Based upon Numbers 16:1–16

Moses vs. Korach

Korach (snarling with contempt): By appointing your brother, Aaron, as High Priest, *you have gone too far! For all the community are holy, every one of them, and because God dwells in their midst, each of them can make the sacred offerings. Why do you and Aaron raise yourselves above God's congregation?*

Moses: *Hear me, sons of Levi. Is it not enough for you that the God of Israel has set you apart from the community of Israel and given you access to the Divine, to perform the duties of God's Tabernacle and to minister to the community and serve them?*

Korach (smirking): No. Our rights have been usurped.

Moses (realizing Korach's intention): *You seek the priesthood, too!* God has commanded each action I have taken; your rebellion, therefore, is not against me. *Truly, it is against the Merciful One that you and all your company have banded together.*

Korach: You think you are the only chosen one. We too are chosen.

Moses (exuding confidence): In the morning, you and your followers bring an offering to the Almighty. Aaron will do the same. God will only accept the offering of the legitimate High Priest. *The man whom the Creator chooses, he shall be the holy one.*

Korach: We shall do as you say.

Suddenly, Moses is accosted by Dathan and Abiram.

Dathan and Abiram (challenging Moses' political leadership): *Is it not enough that you brought us from a land flowing with milk and honey to have us die in the wilderness? Shall you lord it over us?*

Moses (calmly): God has chosen me to lead. Keep the faith, like Joshua and Caleb.

Dathan and Abiram: No, now God chooses us.

Moses (aware that God's wrath will destroy them and their followers, he pleads with the community): *Turn away, I beg you, from near the tents of these wicked men, and touch nothing that belongs to them, for if you do, you will perish with them for all their sins.*

Cross Examination

Korach bases his complaint against Moses on a democratic principle, namely, that the whole community should perform the functions of the priesthood because the entire community is holy. **What do you think of Korach's argument? Is there an element of elitism in Moses' choice of Aaron and his family?** _____

_____

_____

Should certain positions of authority be restricted to an elite group? _____

_____

What are the advantages of elitism? The disadvantages? _____

_____

_____

_____

Competing Values

All humans are created in God's image and entitled to respect, כְּבוֹד הַבְּרִיּוֹת (*kavod habriot*). Therefore, no one should have access to power or prestige in a way that another person does not.

Leadership, מַנְהִיגוּת (*manhigut*), is reserved for those who can carry out their responsibilities guided by the highest moral values and the welfare of the community.

Debate It

The responsibilities of leadership require exceptional skills. Moreover, the power that comes with leadership provides tempting opportunities for self-enrichment. Therefore, some argue that leaders must not only be the best and the brightest, but should also be held to a higher moral standard than average citizens. Others say that leaders, like all people, are imperfect; therefore, leadership should be open to one and all.

Resolved: that leadership should be reserved for an elite class of people who demonstrate exceptional intelligence and adhere to a higher moral standard than those they lead.

Reflections

Moses left Pharaoh's palace and "…went out to his kinfolk and witnessed their labors." (Exodus 2:11). Going out to his people was Moses' first step toward leadership and makes him a role model for us.

Choose a leader whom you admire. List the qualities that make/made that person a good leader.

Which qualities do you share with the leader you admire? Which qualities do you lack?

Create a plan to improve your own leadership skills.

What Would You Do?

You have been a member of a neighborhood club for seven years. When you joined, all members in good standing voted on whom would be invited to join the group. This democratic process created a racially diverse group that included African-Americans, Whites, Asians, and Hispanics. In addition, club members came from all economic classes. Parents, teachers, and local officials admired your accomplishments, and you and your friends attributed much of the club's success to its diversity. During the last four years, however, a small group of unruly kids have voted to invite their like-minded friends, many of whom are violent and aggressive. What began as a small group of troublemakers has grown to a small majority. This year, three of the new members were arrested for destroying property in the neighborhood.

Police have blamed your club. The president and vice-president of the club, who have voted regularly against all the candidates that the agitators have suggested, decided to change the membership process. Instead of the democratic method, they created a committee of only straight-A students to choose whom should be invited to the club. You do not qualify for the committee. Not surprisingly, many members object to such an elite group making all the decisions, and they are threatening to quit. **What would you do?**

CHAPTER 3

The Five Daughters & the Twelve Tribes

Women in the Torah	**1813 B.C.E.**	**1650 B.C.E.**
	Sarah — Abraham's wife. Sarah is an independent woman who seizes the initiative to determine her family's future. • "Whatever Sarah tells you to do, listen to her" (God to Abraham in Genesis 21:12).	**Rebekah** — Isaac's wife. Like Sarah, Rebekah controls her family's destiny. She instructs Jacob to trick Isaac and receive his blessing. • "Your curse, my son, be upon me. Just do as I say..." (Rebekah to Isaac in Genesis 27:13).

Who Is Included?

> ## The plea of Zelophehad's daughters is just.... The plea of the Josephite tribe is just.
>
> (Moses to the Israelites,
> Numbers 27:7, 36:5)

After 39 years of wandering in the wilderness—a wandering filled with rebellions, plagues, and disappointments—the Children of Israel finally camped at the doorstep of the Promised Land. At God's direction, Moses organized a new census. Rumors spread throughout the camp that the census would determine how the Land would be divided. Large tribes, like Judah and Issachar, would receive more land than the smaller tribes, like Simeon and Ephraim. Because the process seemed fair, the people set aside their petty jealousies, and an exhausted jubilation swept through the camp.

In one tent, however, fear, anger, and resentment simmered. The daughters of Zelophehad (*Tz'lafhad*) huddled to discuss their fate. Their father had died along the way, and because he had no sons to inherit his property, the family would lose its entitlement to a portion of the Land. Enraged by an unfair biblical law that denied them equal rights and threatened to leave them homeless, the unmarried women decided to challenge Moses, the High Priest, the Chieftains, and the entire assembly.

1560 B.C.E.

Rachel — Jacob's wife. Tradition regards her as a role model of tenderness and imagines that her tears of mourning for her exiled children awakened God's compassion. • "Restrain your voice from weeping...declares God...Your children will return to their country" (Jeremiah 31:16).

1560 B.C.E.

Leah — Jacob's wife. Leah is mother of six of Jacob's twelve sons, who became the twelve tribes of Israel. • Leah and her sister Rachel are referred to as the matriarchs "who built up the House of Israel" (Ruth 4:11).

1300 B.C.E.

Miriam — Moses' sister. Miriam is the first woman in the Torah to be called a prophet, and the book of Micah gives her equal status alongside Moses and Aaron. • "I redeemed you from the house of bondage, and sent before you Moses, Aaron, and Miriam" (Micah 6:4).

Clarification

1 Why do you think ancient civilizations—including the society built by our biblical ancestors—denied women inheritance rights? _____

_____

_____

_____

2 How do you reconcile Miriam's prominence in the community with the lowly status of women in ancient Israel? _____

_____

_____

_____

_____

_____

3 A popular midrash contrasts the difference between the men and women who wandered in the wilderness: "The fervent longing of these women [Zelophehad's daughters] to have a share in the Holy Land shows how much better and more pious were the women of this generation than the men. The men said, 'Let us make a captain and return to Egypt' (Numbers 14:4). But Israel's women insisted 'Give us a possession in the Land.' (Numbers 27:4). **What does this midrash say about the status of women?**

_____

_____

_____

_____

The Great Debate

Based on Numbers 27:1–11 and 36:1–12

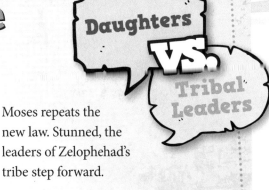

Daughters (emerging from their tent, they march to the Tent of Meeting): *Our father died in the wilderness. He was not one of Korach's faction, which banded together against God, but [he] died for his own sin; and he has left no sons. Let not our father's name be lost to his clan just because he had no son. Give us a holding among our father's kinsmen.*

Moses (shocked by their daring but quickly realizing the complaint is legitimate): Your request is understandable, but I can't make this decision alone.

God (to Moses): *The plea of Zelophehad's daughters is just; give them a hereditary holding among their father's kinsmen; transfer their father's share to them.*

Moses (to the daughters): We will allow you to inherit your father's possession.

Daughters (hugging each other): Thank you. The decision honors our father's memory.

Moses turns aside, as if listening to an internal voice.

God (to Moses): *Further, speak to the Israelite people as follows: If a man dies without leaving a son, you shall transfer his property to his daughter.*

Moses repeats the new law. Stunned, the leaders of Zelophehad's tribe step forward.

Tribal Leaders: *God has commanded to assign the share [of land] of our kinsman Zelophehad to his daughters. But, if they marry persons from another Israelite tribe, their share will be cut off from our ancestral portion and be added to the portion of the tribe into which they marry. Thus our portion will be diminished.*

Moses: You're right. The law states that if a woman marries outside her tribe, she becomes part of her husband's household, and her rights are transferred to his. Let me consult God.

Tribal Leaders: We seek only justice.

Moses: *The plea of the Josephite tribe is just. This is what the Holy One has commanded concerning the daughters of Zelophehad: They may marry anyone they wish, provided they marry into a clan of their father's tribe. No inheritance of the Israelites may pass over from one tribe to another.*

Cross Examination

The Tent of Meeting (*Mishkan*) was sacred ground, where God's presence dwelled. Aaron's sons, Nadav and Avihu, were killed for violating the sanctity of that space. (Leviticus 10:1–2). **What emotions or personal values propelled the sisters to risk their lives and appear there uninvited?** _____

_____

_____

If Zelophehad's daughters had lost their inheritance in the land, what consequences might they have faced? _____

_____

_____

What makes you feel a part of the Jewish community? What are the advantages and disadvantages of affiliating with the Jewish community? _____

_____

_____

Competing Values

Because all human beings are created in the image of God, בְּצֶלֶם אֱלֹהִים (*b'tzelem Elohim*), we are obligated to treat everyone with love and respect.

Although the rights of individuals are important in Judaism, the welfare of the community, קְהִילָה (*kehilah*), and respect for communal norms often take precedence.

Debate It

Immigration reform divides Americans. Those who demand the arrest and deportation of undocumented workers argue that illegal aliens hurt American communities by taking jobs from legal residents and straining communal resources, such as health care and education. Some have estimated the cost at approximately $113 billion a year. Advocates of comprehensive immigration reform disagree. They claim that denying social services to illegal aliens is not only unethical, but also violates the U.S. Constitution.

Resolved: that children of undocumented workers are entitled to public education.

Reflections

Hillel's famous saying urges us to balance personal needs with the needs of the community: "…if I am only for myself, what am I?"

Describe an instance when you sacrificed personal needs for your school or family's needs. **How did you feel?**

American society prizes individual rights. In contrast, Judaism usually places communal needs above personal needs. **Which approach do you prefer? Why?**

Echoes from the Past

Ruth Bader Ginsburg | Associate Justice, U.S. Supreme Court

On the morning of October 19, 1971, Ruth Bader Ginsburg stood with a colleague before the U.S. Supreme Court, ready to argue a case. A petite woman with bookish, gentle features, Ginsburg eyed the nine male justices who would hear her arguments against the state of Idaho. Her client, Sally Reed, had been denied the right to administer her deceased son's estate. Instead of approving Ms. Reed's petition to administer the estate, authorities approved her ex-husband's request because an Idaho law stipulated that "males must be preferred to females" in appointing administrators of estates.

Ginsburg, who was the co-founder of and chief litigator for the Women's Rights Project at the American Civil Liberties Union, had waited years for this case. She believed that the 14th Amendment, which guarantees equal protection under the law, should be applied to gender discrimination cases, even though the Supreme Court had never done so in over 100 years of litigation. In fact, the high court had upheld bans on female lawyers in 1873, on women bartenders in 1948, and on women serving jury duty in 1961.

Ginsburg's argument that day changed history. In a unanimous ruling, the justices recognized that any law that discriminates against women is unconstitutional.

When she was nominated for the Supreme Court in 1993, Ruth Bader Ginsburg acknowledged the important role her mother had played in her life. She was "the bravest and strongest person I have known," Ginsburg said. "I pray that I may be all that she would have been had she lived in an age when women could aspire and achieve, and daughters are cherished as much as sons."

1813–1523 B.C.E.	**1546 B.C.E.**	**1313 B.C.E.**	**1272 B.C.E.**
Abraham, Isaac, Jacob, Sarah, Rebekah, Rachel, and Leah — Our ancestors whom we call upon daily in the Amidah prayer.	**Joseph and slavery in Egypt** — During centuries of enslavement, the Hebrews maintained their tribal identity.	**Moses and the Exodus** — History's most famous rallying cry: "Let My people go." (Exodus 7:16)	**Conquest of Canaan** — Led by Joshua, Moses' hand-picked successor, the often brutal conquest is recounted in the Book of Joshua.

Should We Blow the Whistle?

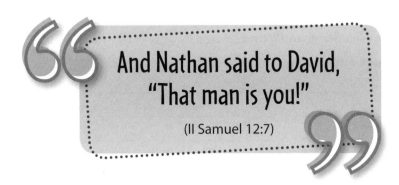

> ## And Nathan said to David, "That man is you!"
>
> (II Samuel 12:7)

King David pushed the pesky thought out of his mind and returned to the work that lay before him. Within minutes, however, the troubling thought wormed its way back into his mind: "Kill him." Recoiling at his own brutality, David chided himself, "Don't compound one horrible mistake with another. Isn't it bad enough that my immoral behavior with Batsheva, Uriah's wife, has left her pregnant?"

Although guilt had been gnawing at his conscience, another equally powerful emotion now seized him: shame. "If the people discover my sin," David worried, "how can I ever stand before them again?"

Without realizing it, King David succumbed to the fear of humiliation and dishonor. He resigned himself to avoid disgrace at all costs. The pesky thought that once flitted innocently into his mind soon became the basis of a consuming, face-saving strategy: "Send Batsheva's husband, Uriah, to the front lines of battle, where, unprotected, he will surely die."

And so the deed was done. The king quickly married Batsheva, Uriah's widow. "But God was displeased with David, and the Almighty sent Nathan, a prophet, to David" (II Samuel 12:1).

1227 B.C.E.	879 B.C.E.	877 B.C.E.	836 B.C.E.
Judges — Twelve heroic leaders who settled disputes among the Israelites and led them in battle against enemies.	**Saul anointed king** — The people demand a king "to govern us like all other nations" (I Samuel 8:5). Samuel, the aging judge at the time, resists, but God commands him to heed the people's demand.	**King David's reign** — The greatest king of Israel, who established Jerusalem as the capital of the Jewish people.	**King Solomon's reign** — David's son, who built the First Temple in Jerusalem. By the end of his reign, however, the people resented the high taxes he levied for his building campaigns.

Clarification

1 **What sin does King David fear the people will discover?**

_____

_____

2 King David's behavior causes guilt, humiliation, and shame. **If each of these emotions could be depicted by an animal, what animals do you think would represent them? Explain your choices.**

_____

_____

_____

_____

3 Judaism understands the agony of psychological pain. In fact, Jewish law says that people who embarrass others in public lose their share in the world to come, while those who commit murder do not. **What do you think of this?**_____

_____

_____

_____

_____

4 **What does the phrase, "and so the deed was done," mean?**

_____

_____

_____

_____

The Great Debate

Nathan VS. David

Nathan (calmly and with no hint of his true purpose): Let me tell you a true story.

David (casually): *I'm listening.*

Nathan (stepping forward and speaking intensely): *There were two men in the same city, one rich and one poor. The rich man had very large flocks and herds, but the poor man had only one little lamb. He cared for it, and it grew up with him and his children.… One day, a traveler came to the rich man. But the rich man did not want to take anything from his own flock to feed the guest. So he stole the poor man's lamb instead.*

David (flying into a rage): *The man who did this deserves to die! And he should pay for the lamb four times over, since he stole it and showed no pity.*

Nathan (leaping forward and pointing his finger at the king): *That man is you!*

David: *What are you talking about? I'm the king!*

Nathan: *Thus says the God of Israel: It was I who anointed you king over Israel…and gave you everything you have. Why then have you flouted the command of the Holy One and done what displeases him? You have put Uriah to the sword; you took his wife and made her your wife and had him killed.*

David stumbles backward, surprised that his sin has been revealed.

Nathan: God will punish you. *The sword shall never depart from your house. I will make a calamity rise against you from within your own house. You acted in secret, but God will make this happen in the sight of all Israel and in broad daylight.*

David (more composed): *I stand guilty before God.*

Nathan: *You shall not die. But the child about to be born to you shall die.*

33

Cross Examination

Why did Nathan begin his confrontation with a parable? _____

_____

What do you think might have happened if Nathan had confronted King David immediately? _____

_____

_____

Do you think Nathan understood beforehand what the consequences of confronting the king might have been? If so, why do you think he undertook the task?

_____

What personal characteristic does Nathan exhibit?

_____

What personal characteristic does King David exhibit? _____

Competing Values

It takes courage, אוֹמֶץ לֵב (*ometz lev*), to stand up to authority and express one's convictions.

Talebearing, לֹא תֵלֵךְ רָכִיל בְּעַמֶּיךָ (*lo talech rachil b'amecha*), which has been identified with revealing secrets, is prohibited in the Torah.

Debate It

Called the cornerstone of democracy, the people's right to free speech and a free press is guaranteed by the First Amendment. At times, however, government agencies and private enterprises have legitimate rights to secrecy. For example, national security operations frequently demand strict secrecy, and private companies have a right to protect information, like recipes and formulas. On the other hand, blowing the whistle on corrupt government actions and business decisions that threaten the general welfare of society is not only legal, but also virtuous.

Resolved: that the U.S. judicial system give preference to truth-seeking at the expense of classified information or privileged communications.

Reflections

The Torah commands us to reprimand wrongdoers (Leviticus 19:17). At times that obligation conflicts with the requirement to avoid revealing secrets.

How can secrets be helpful in a relationship? How can they be harmful?

Judaism prohibits revealing secrets, even if no one will be hurt. **Under what circumstances would you reveal a friend's secret?**

Case Study

391 U.S. 563 (1968)

United States Supreme Court

Pickering v. Board of Education

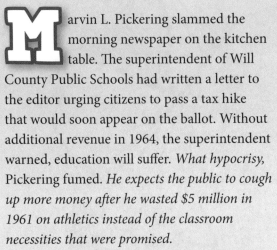

Marvin L. Pickering slammed the morning newspaper on the kitchen table. The superintendent of Will County Public Schools had written a letter to the editor urging citizens to pass a tax hike that would soon appear on the ballot. Without additional revenue in 1964, the superintendent warned, education will suffer. *What hypocrisy*, Pickering fumed. *He expects the public to cough up more money after he wasted $5 million in 1961 on athletics instead of the classroom necessities that were promised.*

Pickering, a teacher at East High School, paced around the room. *Someone has to tell the public the truth*, he thought. As he sat to write a response to the letter, he remembered the superintendent's warning: "Any teacher who opposes the referendum should be prepared for the consequences." Gripping the pen tightly, Pickering accused the school board of ignoring the promises it made during the last election. "To sod football fields on borrowed money and then not be able to pay teachers' salaries is

getting the cart before the horse," he charged. "The taxpayers were really taken to the cleaners." Fearing he might be fired for blowing the whistle, Pickering added, "I must sign this letter as a citizen, taxpayer, and voter, not as a teacher, since that freedom has been taken from the teachers by the administration. Do you really know what goes on behind those stone walls at the high school?"

The school board fired Pickering after his letter appeared. Officials claimed that his charges were false and "detrimental to the efficient operation and administration of the schools of the district." Pickering asserted that his First Amendment right to freedom of speech had been violated.

The Supreme Court ruled in Pickering's favor, saying, "Absent proof of false statements knowingly or recklessly made by him, a teacher's exercise of his right to speak on issues of public importance may not furnish the basis for his dismissal from public employment."

63 B.C.E.	37 B.C.E.	4 B.C.E.	39 C.E.
Romans occupy Judea	Herod, an Idumean whose family was forcibly converted to Judaism by the Hasmoneans, is appointed king by the Romans.	Direct Roman rule begins after Herod's death and the ousting of his four sons, who ruled briefly after him.	Emperor Caligula demands that idols be erected in the Temple.

Is Extremism Ever Justified?

> ## My children, why do you destroy this city and why do you seek to burn the Temple?
>
> (Yochanan ben Zakkai to the Zealots
> in Avot d'Rabbi Natan 4:5)

Emperor Caligula stared down from his throne at the delegation of Jews from the troublesome province of Judea. "Fools," he shrieked. "You alone in the entire Roman Empire refuse to erect my statue in your Holy Temple." Spittle dripped from his gaping mouth and rolled down his chin. The Jews noticed that the madman made no effort to wipe it away. "I should execute you instantly and destroy your worthless little country," he howled.

Before Caligula could punish the Jewish people in Judea, an assassin killed him in 41 C.E. His death inspired the Zealots, a political party in Judea that urged armed resistance against Roman rule. Crushed by excessive taxes, the people of Judea finally revolted in 66 C.E. "We must fight now," said Abba Sikra, leader of the radical Zealots, "even if it means certain death."

Yochanan ben Zakkai, a renowned Torah sage, opposed Sikra and the Zealots. Ben Zakkai counseled peace, arguing that a compromise might bring heavier taxes and religious restrictions, but at least Judaism would survive.

Zealots and moderates argued about the best response to the crisis. Unfortunately, their squabbling erupted into physical violence and civil war.

66 C.E.	66–68 C.E.	68 C.E.	70 C.E.
Roman governor loots silver from the Temple, inciting Jewish riots, which meet with initial success. • Early success inspires Zealots, and their influence grows.	Roman army crushes Jewish radicals in Galilee, and the survivors flee to Jerusalem.	Roman General Vespasian besieges Jerusalem. • Civil war between Zealots and moderates erupts in Jerusalem. Yochanan ben Zakkai escapes and establishes Yavneh.	Jerusalem and Second Temple completely destroyed. Jewish people exiled.

Clarification

1 A zealot is an extremist. **When, if ever, is extremism justified?**

_____
_____
_____
_____

2 **How should a nation decide when it is appropriate to go to war?**
_____

_____
_____
_____

3 **What motivates some people to become pacifists and others to become military extremists?** _____
_____
_____
_____

4 Judaism considers human life sacred, and yet, we are obligated to protect ourselves from aggressors intent on killing us. The law also obligates us to intervene when we see a lethal aggressor attacking someone else. **Do you agree with the principle of self-defense outlined in the Torah and Talmud? Is it fair that Jewish law requires us to intervene if we are only onlookers to a violent attack?** _____

_____
_____
_____

The Great Debate

Ben Zakkai VS. Abba Sikra

Based on stories recounted in the Talmud (Gittin 56a–b) and the Midrash (Avot d'Rabbi Natan 1.5, Lamentations Rabbah 1:5, and Ecclesiastes Rabbah 7:12).

Abba Sikra: As you have heard, I ordered that the storehouses of food inside the walls of Jerusalem be burnt. We must fight the Romans at all costs. If it takes starving our countrymen to make them fight, so be it.

Ben Zakkai: *Woe!*

Abba Sikra: *Why do you make that exclamation?*

Ben Zakkai: *Because so long as the stores were intact, the people would not expose themselves to the dangers of battle. Now that you are starving them, they will be become desperate, and they will fight.*

Abba Sikra: That is exactly what we intend.

Ben Zakkai: *My children, why do you destroy this city and why do you seek to burn the Temple?* For that is what Vespasian will do if you rise up against him.

Abba Sikra: We bow only to God, not to a Roman, be he a general or an emperor.

Ben Zakkai: *What is it that Vespasian asks of you? In truth, he asks nothing of you save one bow or one arrow, and then he will leave you alone.* The tribute tax he requires is a small price to pay.

Abba Sikra: *Even as we went forth against the two generals before him and slew them, so we shall go forth against him and slay him.*

Ben Zakkai: You are making a terrible mistake, and the people will suffer. *Be not in haste to pull down the high places of the Gentiles, lest you have to rebuild them with your own hand. It is written that thou shall build the altar of unhewn stones, and shall lift up no iron tools upon them. If these stones are meant to make peace between Israel and God, then they are also meant to make peace between man and wife, family and family, city and city, nation and nation, and between government and government.*

Cross Examination

Jewish tradition blames the Temple's destruction on the unfounded hatred (*sinat chinam*) between Zealots and moderates. **What do you think?**

_____

_____

_____

What would you say to convince Abba Sikra to adopt a different strategy? To Ben Zakkai?

_____

_____

_____

In Deuteronomy 20:8, the Torah says that prior to battle, officials assembled the people and asked, "Is there anyone afraid and disheartened? Let him go back to his home, lest the courage of his comrades flag like his." **Contrast this approach with the Zealots' approach to preparing for battle. Which is more effective?** _____

_____

_____

Debate It

Judaism cherishes peace; indeed, the Talmud considers destroying a human life the equivalent of destroying the entire world. And yet, Jewish law recognizes that the pursuit of peace must be set aside when the life of the nation is threatened. Although self-defense is regarded as a just reason to kill an enemy, the Torah curbs excessive brutality with a series of laws meant to limit violence on the battlefield.

Resolved: that the nation's survival justifies the use of any and all means of warfare.

Competing Values

Two conflicting values emerge in this debate: the obligation to pursue peace, רוֹדֵף שָׁלוֹם (*rodef shalom*), and the requirement to defend oneself against an aggressor, מִלְחֶמֶת חוֹבָה (*milchemet chovah*).

Reflections

The book of Ecclesiastes says there is a time for everything, including, "a time for war and a time for peace."

Under what circumstances would you enlist to fight for your country?

Is compulsory military service, such as a draft system, fair?

Describe a time when you were zealous about something. **How did you feel? How was your behavior received?**

What Would You Do?

 U.S. citizen, known as Suspect A, has regularly spread hatred of America in speeches broadcast on radical Web sites. The government has evidence that several terrorist attacks carried out against America were motivated by these hate-filled rants; moreover, prosecutors suspect that Suspect A had a direct relationship with the terrorists being held for those attacks. The government wants to find and arrest Suspect A, but he has fled to a foreign country, where it is difficult to arrest him.

CIA intelligence has tracked Suspect A's activity and uncovered several plots against America that involve him. At last, the suspect's location is uncovered. Officials recommend assassinating Suspect A with a missile fired from an unmanned airplane. Others, however, counsel that Suspect A is an American citizen and entitled to a fair trial. **What would you do?**

200 B.C.E. – 350 C.E.	190 B.C.E. – 350 C.E.	140 B.C.E. – 70 C.E.
The Sanhedrin was Judaism's supreme legislative and judicial assembly.	High Priest's leadership eclipsed. Sanhedrin run by *Nasi* (President) and *Av Beit Din* (Head of the Court).	Pharisees and Sadducees advocate competing schools of thought on social and religious matters.

How Do We Interpret the Law?

> **Both are the words of the living God...but the law is in agreement with Beit Hillel.**
>
> (Talmud: Eruvin 13b)

"God appointed us—the Levites—to bless the people, decide their disputes, and serve the Almighty in the Holy Temple," protested the old man. "It has been so since we wandered in the wilderness."

"You're right, Simon," replied the lanky Sage, calmly sipping his tea. "But those days are far behind us. Our people need laws for today's world." The Sage stared deeply into his host's eyes, probing for the friendship they once shared. Sadly, he found only bitterness. The split between their approaches to Jewish law seemed unbridgeable.

"The laws of God are eternal," snapped Simon. "You can't make up things that aren't written in the Torah."

The visitor put down his cup. An air of confidence settled over him, as if he had won this debate many times. "We follow the written Torah, Simon. But you can't ignore the great Sages, beginning with Moses, who interpreted our laws and applied them to every imaginable situation in life. The people need the oral law as a guide to living."

"Nonsense!" Simon barked. "You and your followers have usurped the Sanhedrin's authority."

100 B.C.E.	50 B.C.E.	200 C.E. – 500 C.E.
Rabbi Hillel born in Babylonia. After Hillel, the President of the Sanhedrin will always descend from School of Hillel.	Rabbi Shammai born in Eretz Yisrael.	Rabbis of the Talmud follow decisions of School of Hillel.

Clarification

1 Simon, the fictional character in the vignette, represents the Sadducees. He says that God's laws are eternal. **What does he mean?**

_____

_____

_____

2 Simon's guest, who represents the Pharisees, states that laws must be interpreted and applied to "every imaginable situation in life." **How is his viewpoint different from Simon's?** _____

_____

_____

_____

3 **Is it appropriate to interpret a law in ways that were never intended when the law was written? What are the risks of doing so? What are the advantages?** _____

_____

_____

_____

4 Today, we use the term "originalist" to describe judges who refuse to interpret laws in ways that were not intended when the law first appeared. During Hillel and Shammai's era (first century B.C.E.), originalists were called Sadducees and their opponents were called Pharisees. **Which judicial philosophy appeals to you?**

_____

_____

_____

The Great Debate

Beit Shammai VS. Beit Hillel

This imaginary debate, based on several well-known stories in the Talmud, captures the two approaches to Jewish law depicted in the fictitious vignette on page 41. Hillel, who presided over the great Sanhedrin in the first century of the Common Era, embraced the liberal interpretation of Torah law. His opponent, Shammai, was known for his strict interpretation of the law.

Beit Shammai: A non-Jew came to me and had the nerve to say, *"I will convert to Judaism if you teach me the whole Torah while I stand on one foot."* Imagine the stupidity of such a request. I immediately dismissed him.

Beit Hillel: I'm sorry you pushed him away. He came to me afterwards, and I told him, *"What is hateful to you, do not do to your neighbor. That is the whole Torah; the rest is commentary. Now go and study!"*

Beit Shammai: We learn from our teacher that you must be strict and honest. *Suppose a bride is lame or blind. Should one say about her, "Oh, what a lovely and graceful bride?" No, because the Torah warns us against lying. You should describe her as she actually is.*

Beit Hillel: We learn from our teacher that you must be lenient and compassionate. *Surely, it is more considerate that praise be spoken at such a time.*

Beit Shammai: The strict and correct way to light the Chanukah menorah is this: *On the first day, eight candles are lit and thereafter they are reduced by one each day.*

Beit Hillel: The way to light the candles that makes the most sense is this: *On the first day, one candle is lit and thereafter they are increased each day.*

Beit Shammai: Our custom is correct because the candles represent the oil, which became less and less. The candles also represent the days of the holiday, which too become less and less.

Beit Hillel: We believe our custom is correct because the candles represent the miracle of light, which became greater and greater each day. *One should only increase in matters of holiness and celebration, not decrease.*

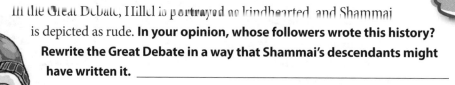

Cross Examination

In the Great Debate, Hillel is portrayed as kindhearted, and Shammai is depicted as rude. **In your opinion, whose followers wrote this history? Rewrite the Great Debate in a way that Shammai's descendants might have written it.** _____

_____

Shammai lived a privileged life, filled with wealth and luxuries. Hillel, on the other hand, lived in poverty. **Do you think the Sages' socioeconomic status affected the way they interpreted the law? Do you think the socioeconomic status of today's judges and legislators affects their actions?** _____

_____

Imagine that the people listed below had lived during the time of Hillel and Shammai. **Which Sage do you think they would have followed? Your father? Your mother? Your teacher? Your U.S. senators? Your rabbi? The president of the United States?** _____

_____

Competing Values

Religious authority rests upon the concept of תּוֹרָה מִן הַשָּׁמַיִם (*Torah min ha-shamayim*), the understanding that God revealed at Mount Sinai all the laws that guide Jewish life.

On the other hand, the oral tradition, תּוֹרָה שֶׁבְּעַל פֶּה (*Torah she b'al-peh*), allows beliefs and principles that are not in the Torah to become authoritative.

Debate It

Like the debate between the Pharisees and Sadducees centuries ago, a controversy between competing judicial philosophies brews today. Conservative judges embrace the idea of original intent, which demands that judicial decisions be based only on the original intent of a law. Advocates of original intent warn that judges who broadly interpret the law are creating new laws and trespassing on legislative authority. Liberal judges, on the other hand, believe that laws must be continually interpreted to accommodate social and technological change over time. Otherwise, they warn, laws become outdated and irrelevant to the lives of citizens.

Resolved: that judges should consider only the original intent of a law.

Reflections

Religious authority must be grounded first in our personal recognition of God as the Divine source of creation.

What institutions have civil and moral authority over your life? How do these institutions acquire their authority?

What are the advantages of having clearly defined sources of authority?

Do you believe God revealed laws and commandments at Sinai? If so, do you think the laws are eternal, or can they be changed? And if they can be changed, who has the authority to change them?

Echoes from the Past

Judah Ha-Nasi (135–219 C.E.)

Tomb of Judah Ha-Nasi, Beit Shearim, Israel

"The cool air of Tzippori comforts my stomach pain," Rabbi Judah explained to the visitor who had asked why the Sage had moved his *beit din* (Jewish court) from Beit Shearim.

A smile spread upon the visitor's lips, though he dared not utter the thought that crossed his mind: *Ah, the stories of his flatulence are true. How fortunate I am to visit him here!*

Rabbi Judah instinctively understood the reason for the man's cryptic smile. "Trouble comes to the world only on account of the unlearned," he mused. With a nod of his head, the Sanhedrin's leader summoned a guard to escort the visitor out of the receiving room.

As the man exited, a disciple approached the rabbi. "*Rabbeinu ha-kadosh* (our holy teacher), the *beit din* awaits you."

Judah rose and strode into the hall where his students had gathered. They rose to greet him.

"What case are we hearing?" he asked.

"The communities of Beit Shean, Caesarea, and Kefar Zemah ask to be released from paying tithes on their crops."

"What prompts their request?"

"They dwell in poverty, Rabbi."

The furrows in Judah's brow deepened. "Let us see if the law can accommodate them."

The rabbis debated the issue and finally settled into two opposing camps: Those who advocated the strict opinion—called *machmir*—refused the request because the Torah clearly says, "for it is the tithes set aside by the Israelites as a gift to God that I give to the Levites as their share."

Rabbi Judah led the lenient group—called *meikil*—that argued in favor of releasing the poor communities from the tithes. "The obligation," he said, "only falls on communities within Eretz Yisrael. Let us exclude them from the sanctity of the Land." His opinion was accepted.

Rabbi Judah Ha-Nasi compiled and wrote down the legal interpretations of the Torah known as the oral law. His masterful work, which is called the Mishnah, preserved, cultivated, and applied Torah law to modern life—a process that continues today.

CHAPTER 7

The Vilna Gaon & the Ba'al Shem Tov

1648–1654	**1660**	**1698**
Violent pogroms by Cossacks in Ukraine against Polish gentry and Jews creates a yearning for redemption.	Shabbetai Zvi claims to be the messiah and gains widespread acceptance. When he is arrested by authorities, he converts to Islam.	Birth of Israel ben Eliezer, the Ba'al Shem Tov—sometimes called by the acronym *Besht*.

How Can We Connect with God?

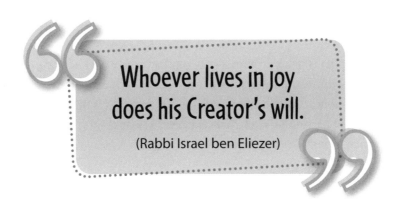

> **Whoever lives in joy does his Creator's will.**
>
> (Rabbi Israel ben Eliezer)

To Yaakov, the *beit midrash* (study hall) seemed like a noisy marketplace filled with undecipherable syllables. When he entered the room, he felt as if a part of him were dying. "I feel closer to God when I'm wandering in the forest, surrounded by God's creation," he confided to his *chevruta* (study partner).

"Don't say those words around me," his partner replied, a look of horror spreading across his face. "I don't want to be excommunicated."

"What do you mean?" stammered Yaakov.

"Don't you know what's happening? Our yeshiva supports the *mitnagdim*, the movement launched by the Vilna Gaon against the Ba'al Shem Tov."

"There's a movement against the *Besht* and the Chasidim?" Yaakov asked, his voice rising in anger. "All we want is to rejoice in the Almighty's presence; to cling to God in a state of loving attachment." Yaakov stopped speaking, realizing that the word "we" had carelessly slipped off his tongue.

An angry murmur spread throughout the hall. Its vehemence pierced the religious fervor that had swept over Yaakov. When he realized that everyone was staring at him, Yaakov tried to run, but his feet wouldn't move. He felt his face burning from embarrassment as he collapsed on the floor.

1720
Birth of Rabbi Eliyahu of Vilna, the Vilna Gaon (genius)

1734
Chasidism emerges as a movement that emphasizes personal connection to God through simple acts of joyful celebration.

1770
The Jewish Enlightenment (Haskalah) arises, emphasizing integration into the broader society and pursuit of science and secular studies.

Clarification

1 Why do some Jews feel closer to God when they study Torah?

_____

_____

_____

2 The prophet Isaiah saw angels serving God while the Creator sat on a heavenly throne. In his vision, Isaiah heard the angels chanting, "Holy, holy, holy, is the God of Hosts; the whole world is filled with God's glory" (Isaiah 6:3). **How does this verse support the religious preference to seek God in the forest?**_____

_____

_____

3 Can you find a verse in the Torah that supports the religious preference to seek God through study? _____

_____

_____

4 Are these two spiritual paths incompatible? Which approach do you prefer? _____

_____

_____

5 Historical events often influence religious perspectives. **How did the pogroms of 1648 and the apostasy of the false messiah Shabbetai Zvi influence the conflict between the Ba'al Shem Tov and the Vilna Gaon?** _____

_____

_____

The Great Debate

There is no record that the Vilna Gaon and the Ba'al Shem Tov ever met, though their followers clashed repeatedly. This debate, therefore, is purely imaginary.

Ba'al Shem Tov: No matter what circumstances afflict us, God is very close. The best way to find God is to pray with complete concentration and joy. *Whoever lives in joy does his Creator's will.*

Vilna Gaon: I agree that God is close to us, but the best way to find God is to study Torah. *Everything that was, is, and will be, is included in the Torah.*

Ba'al Shem Tov: Of course, study is important, but the main purpose of life is to *cling to God and attach oneself to the spirit and light of God.* This is best achieved through prayer, because *the essence of worship is the feeling of oneness with God.*

Vilna Gaon: You're misguided, and your approach threatens Judaism. God's plan for us is laid out in the Torah. The only way to discover God's will, therefore, is to regularly study the holy writings.

Ba'al Shem Tov: *Everything created by God contains a spark of holiness. Moreover, everything we do, such as singing, dancing, and fervent prayer, releases sparks of divinity.*

Vilna Gaon: Beware. You are leading people away from study, away from observing the commandments. You are leading them into sin, and you must be stopped.

Ba'al Shem Tov: No, I am leading them to joy and love and God.

Vilna Gaon: The sages have said, "*Talmud torah k'neged kulam—the study of the law takes precedence over everything.*" That is the way it must be. Who are you to say differently?

Cross Examination

Describe the type of person that the Ba'al Shem Tov's message appeals to, **What about the Vilna Gaon's message?** _____

_____

What evidence can you find in the debate to support your opinions? _____

_____

The Besht and the Vilna Gaon disagree about the purpose of life. Describe their differences. Find evidence in the three paragraphs of the Sh'ma—V'ahavta, V'haya im shamoa, and Vayomer—that supports each man's thinking.

_____

Can you identify modern supporters of the Besht's philosophy? Of the Vilna Gaon's philosophy? _____

_____

Competing Values

Learning Torah, תַּלְמוּד תּוֹרָה (*talmud Torah*), is an affirmation of our spiritual vitality and the way to cement our bond with God. Insights gained through the continuous learning of Torah give meaning to life and provide communal uplift.

Happiness, שִׂמְחָה (*simcha*), is a state of internal satisfaction that derives from trust, faith, confidence, hopefulness, and appreciation of the little things in life.

Debate It

The search to understand the origin and meaning of life has captivated humans since our earliest ancestors looked into the night sky and wondered how the universe began and if they were alone in it. Exploring life's mysteries has developed along two strikingly different paths: scientific investigation of the physical world, which depends on intellectual analysis and human reason, and artistic expression, which relies on personal intuition to discover the truths and emotions we share with others.

Resolved: that the meaning of life and the hidden mysteries of the world lie beyond the realm of scientific study.

✳ The book of Deuteronomy explains that God's will is "not too baffling for you, nor is it beyond reach." (30:11).

Do you feel as if you are performing God's will when you do *mitzvot*? What can you do to cultivate this feeling?

When do you most feel God's presence? What can you do to cultivate an awareness that God is all around you?

Echoes from the Past

Rabbi Adin Steinsaltz

e looked deeply into the doctor's eyes, searching for a glimmer of hope, but Rabbi Adin Steinsaltz found none.

"Operating on your spleen would be like playing Russian roulette," the doctor explained. "I'm not willing to take that risk, and I don't think you should be, either."

Rabbi Steinsaltz stroked his scraggly red beard and gazed out the window. After several minutes, the doctor spoke again.

"Rabbi, did you hear? It's too dangerous to operate."

"Yes, I heard you." Although Steinsaltz was sitting in the doctor's office, his mind—which TIME magazine described as an intellect that appears only once every millennium—was wrestling with a difficult section of Gemara. Since 1965, Rabbi Steinsaltz's dream of translating the Babylonian Talmud into Modern Hebrew, and writing a commentary on all 63 tractates, had consumed him. He refused to allow his declining health to interfere with his goal: helping people understand the Talmud.

"Do you agree with the American doctors who said that my spleen might heal itself?" he whispered.

"No, Rabbi. You have a genetic disease, which might return even if we risk removing your spleen." The doctor's pessimism hung in the air, but Rabbi Steinsaltz chose to ignore it.

"Thank you," he said graciously as he stood to leave. But before he reached the doorway, Rabbi Steinsaltz stopped and smiled to himself; the solution to the difficult text had crystallized in his mind.

"Is there something else?" the doctor asked.

"Yes," the rabbi laughed, "about 38 more volumes to translate and explain."

The Talmud is the central pillar of Jewish knowledge, says Rabbi Steinsaltz, "but it is a book that Jews cannot understand. This is a dangerous situation, like a collective amnesia. I tried to make pathways through which people will be able to enter the Talmud without encountering impassable barriers." Rabbi Steinsaltz completed the project in November 2010.

CHAPTER 8

Spinoza & the Amsterdam Rabbis

1571	1590	1632
Northern provinces of the Netherlands declare independence from Catholic Spain.	Conversos (forced converts to Christianity who secretly remained Jewish) flee Spain and Portugal and flock to Amsterdam.	Baruch Spinoza is born in Amsterdam.

Does Judaism Have Boundaries?

> **But having been unable to reform him, but rather, on the contrary, daily receiving more information about the abominable heresies which he practiced...Spinoza should be excommunicated and expelled from the people of Israel.**
>
> (Amsterdam Jewish Council)

> **I enter gladly on the path that is opened to me.**
>
> (Spinoza)

"Our sources warn us that Baruch Spinoza denies God's existence," whispered the elegantly dressed Dutchman. Though Reuben could not see the speaker's face, he sensed fear in every syllable.

He has an economic interest in solving this problem, Reuben reminded himself.

A hand reached out from the darkness and clutched Reuben's arm. "If church elders feel that Spinoza's views could infect society," he warned, "they'll crack down on the Jewish community. Our business relationships will suffer."

"Who is your source, Diedrick?"

"A friend inside the Catholic church told me that a local priest who spies on conversos sent a letter to Inquisition officials abroad."

Will they never leave these poor people alone? Reuben wondered.

Jews in Spain and Portugal were forced to choose between Christianity or a painful death. Many of them, like Spinoza's family, chose baptism, though they secretly remained Jews.

Fortunately for us, mused Reuben, *large numbers of conversos fled to Amsterdam, where their contributions to the economy have ensured our freedom.*

"It's in our mutual interest to maintain order," Diedrick cautioned. "We prosper together as long as the church doesn't interfere. Don't you agree?"

"Of course. I'll speak with the rabbis. They're already outraged by Spinoza's unorthodox views."

1650		1656
Amsterdam becomes an important international commercial center, where Jewish merchants thrive.	Amsterdam develops a reputation for intellectual foment.	Spinoza is excommunicated from the Jewish community.

Clarification

1 The vignette portrays cooperation between the Amsterdam Jewish community and the city's businesspeople. **How did each side in this alliance benefit from the arrangement?**

_____

_____

_____

_____

2 Diedrick, the fictitious Amsterdam businessman, worries that Spinoza's views might "infect" society. **What does he mean?**

_____

_____

_____

_____

3 Who wields control of Amsterdam society? How do you know?

_____

_____

_____

_____

_____

4 Why would the rabbis in Amsterdam cooperate with the Dutch authorities to silence Spinoza? _____

_____

_____

_____

The Great Debate

Here is the debate between Spinoza and the Amsterdam rabbis in the form of an imagined conversation. While no record of their exchange survives, this debate incorporates language from the Excommunication Notice issued by the Amsterdam Jewish Council (Ma'amad), reports about the trial, and excerpts from Spinoza's books.

Rabbis: *We have long known of your evil opinions and deeds, and have tried by various ways and promises to turn you from these evil ways.*

Spinoza: What am I accused of?

Rabbis: *Daily we receive more information about your abominable heresies,* concerning God, the soul, and the Law.

Spinoza: *The freedom to philosophize and to say what I think…this I want to vindicate completely.*

Rabbis: Is it true you deny that God creates and rules the world? Do you believe that God and nature are the same, and that God exists only in a philosophical sense?

Spinoza: *By God's direction, I mean the fixed and unchanging order of Nature…so it is the same thing whether we say that all things happen according to Nature's law, or that they are regulated by God's decree and direction.*

Rabbis: Is it true that you deny that God blessed humans with a soul and also gave us the Torah?

Spinoza: I hold that everything comes from Nature *and that the method of interpreting the Torah is no different from the method of interpreting Nature.*

Rabbis: Is it true that you deny that the Jews are God's chosen people?

Spinoza: *The individual Jew, taken apart from his social organization and government, possesses no gift of God above other men, and there is no difference between Jew and Gentile….At the present time, therefore, there is absolutely nothing that the Jews can arrogate to themselves beyond other people.*

Rabbis: *You should be excommunicated and expelled from the people of Israel.*

Spinoza: *I enter gladly on the path that is opened to me, with the consolation that my departure will be more innocent than was the Exodus of the early Hebrews from Egypt. This excommunication compels me to nothing which I should not have done in any case.*

Cross Examination

By equating God with nature, Spinoza disavowed a personal God. **What core Jewish beliefs are overturned by Spinoza's view?** _____

_____

Spinoza, who is sometimes called the father of modern science, believed that truth can be discovered by reasoning. **Why would the rabbis of Amsterdam disagree with this?**

_____

How do reason and faith differ? What elements of Judaism are based on faith? On reason? _____

_____

Would Spinoza be excommunicated from Judaism today? Are there any boundaries to membership in today's Jewish community? In other words, are there ideas, behaviors, and affiliations that would put someone outside the community? Should there be boundaries? _____

_____

Debate It

Tension between individual rights and the common good exists in all communities. For society to thrive, citizens must accept certain responsibilities, such as obeying laws, paying taxes, and respecting neighbors. At times, individuals must sacrifice their rights for the good of the whole, such as by obeying "No Smoking" restrictions in restaurants.

Similarly, communal authorities must honor the right of citizens to pursue goals that satisfy them. At times, government must sacrifice the common good to preserve individual rights; for example, by freeing a confessed criminal who was improperly interrogated.

Resolved: that the common good should take precedence over individual liberty.

Competing Values

קְהִילָה (kehilah) — Judaism is a communal religion, and Jews have important obligations toward their communities. The community also has responsibility to each individual member.

בְּחִירָה חָפְשִׁית (bechirah chofsheet) — Judaism affirms each individual's moral freedom to choose.

Reflections

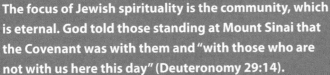

The focus of Jewish spirituality is the community, which is eternal. God told those standing at Mount Sinai that the Covenant was with them and "with those who are not with us here this day" (Deuteronomy 29:14).

Is Judaism too tribal? (Are we too inward-focused?)

Have you ever taken a stand in opposition to normative Jewish beliefs? Explain.

How can you strengthen your attachment to the Jewish community?

How do you conceive of God?

What Would You Do?

As a member of the city council, you are frequently challenged to balance the rights of individual citizens with the needs of the community. For example, the council recently passed a law that requires all students in the school district to be vaccinated before starting school. A group of parents objected, claiming that their parental rights had been violated. It is obvious to you that vaccinations protect students from the spread of contagious diseases, and, therefore, that mandatory vaccination benefits the welfare of the entire community.

But you are not so sure about the case before you now, which pits individual rights against the good of the community. The case involves eminent domain, the right of government to seize private property for public use. Most cases of eminent domain involve road construction. Homeowners are required to accept fair compensation from the government if their homes are in the way of a public road construction project.

The mayor, however, wants to invoke the right of eminent domain to build a large shopping mall that financial experts predict will stimulate the economy. At the least, the owners of the shopping mall will pay more money in property taxes than the current small businesses that occupy the land. The mayor's critics argue that eminent domain cannot be used to take property from one private owner and give it to another private owner simply because it will generate more money for the community. You're being asked to support the mayor. **What would you do?**

1770

Haskalah — This intellectual movement emerges, encouraging Jews to integrate into the broader society and pursue secular studies.

1791

Emancipation — In the aftermath of the French Revolution, France grants Jews full citizenship.

1800–1906

Wissenschaft des Judentum (Jewish science)— Jewish scholars use critical tools to demonstrate that Judaism evolved throughout history.

Tradition or Change?

> **Faith and reason...is the guarantee for [Judaism's] survival.**
>
> (Abraham Geiger)

> **Our slogan is Moderate Reform.**
>
> (Zecharias Frankel)

> **To obliterate the tenets and ordinances of Judaism—is that the Reform we need?**
>
> (Samson Raphael Hirsch)

Elke went to bed every night dreading the arguments between her parents. "Do they think I can't hear them?" she whispered to her cat, Chatuli.

The shouting matches started soon after her mother bought a German translation of the Torah. "Some man who lived a long time ago wrote it," Elke explained to Chatuli. "Vater—I mean *Abbah*—told *Eemah* that reading it would lead to a-a-assim-i-la-tion. I'm not sure what that means, but I think it's bad."

The cat purred quietly until the heated discussion in the dining room began.

"Rabbi Geiger and the reformers are bringing Judaism into the modern age," said her mother. "We'll never be accepted in society if we cling to ancient superstitions. Let the power of reason bloom, Heinrich!"

Elke, who usually agreed with her mother, smiled. "If *Eemah* wins, Chatuli, I will study poetry, philosophy, and even…"

Before she could finish, Elke's father hollered.

"Magda, you're naïve. Can't you see that Rabbi Hirsch is right? The changes you endorse, such as praying in German, will destroy our sacred tradition. It would be better if we had not received our civil rights."

1848	1875	1897	1902
Revolutions of 1848 — Political upheavals urging democratic rights sweep through Europe.	Hebrew Union College , the Reform movement's seminary, is founded in Cincinnati, Ohio.	The Modern Orthodox seminary of Yeshiva University, Rabbi Isaac Elhanan Theological Seminary is founded in New York City.	The Conservative movement's Jewish Theological Seminary in New York City is reorganized.

Clarification

1 **Why would a German translation of the Torah threaten Elke's father?** _____
_____
_____
_____
_____

2 **Why did Elke's father fear assimilation?** _____
_____
_____
_____
_____

3 Elke's mother accused her husband of clinging to superstitions. **What did she mean?** _____
_____
_____
_____
_____
_____

4 **What could prompt Elke's father to say that he would have preferred not to have gained civil rights if emancipation means losing Judaism?** _____
_____
_____
_____
_____

The Great Debate

Here is an imaginary debate between Rabbi Abraham Geiger, leader of the Reform movement, and his opponents, Rabbis Samson Raphael Hirsch and Zecharias Frankel. Rabbi Hirsch founded the Modern Orthodox movement, and Rabbi Frankel created Conservative Judaism. This debate incorporates language from each of the rabbis' sermons, books, and public debates.

Geiger: *For the love of heaven, how much longer can we continue this deceit, to expound the stories from the Bible…over and over again as actual historical happenings, to accept as supernatural events of world import stories which we ourselves have relegated to the realm of legend?*

Hirsch: Would you deny the Torah?

Geiger: I do not deny the Torah. But all laws and all prayers that are unworthy or irrelevant should be eliminated.

Hirsch: *To cut, curtail and obliterate the tenets and ordinances of Judaism —is that the reform we need? To remodel the Divine service in accordance with the demands of the age—is that the reform we desire?*

Geiger: *The course to be taken, my dear fellow, is that of critical study. Judaism need not fear such an unprejudiced critical approach.*

Frankel: *Our slogan is 'moderate reform.' Time hurries onward and radical reforms are demanded, but we do not want to forget that not all demands of our times are justified.*

Geiger: So you agree that both *faith and reason…[are] the guarantee for [Judaism's] survival?*

Frankel: I do, but *so much that is characteristic in Judaism has already been obliterated. For example, I believe that a part of the service be held in German, [but] Hebrew must predominate. Our youth must be taught Hebrew in order to understand the service and the Bible.*

Geiger: And you agree that *from now on no distinction between duties for men and women should be made?*

Hirsch: *When the will of the people is expressed…what authority could deny them this right?*

Cross Examination

The mid-19th century was a period of intellectual and political turmoil. **How were Rabbi Geiger's reforms influenced by the emergence of the scientific process and the call for democratic change? Give examples from the debate.** _____

Rabbi Hirsch speaks contemptuously about changing Judaism to meet "the demands of the age." In his most famous book, *The Nineteen Letters*, Hirsch asked, "Did Judaism ever correspond with the views of dominant contemporaries?" **Give an example from Jewish history to support Rabbi Hirsch's opinion.** _____

Unlike Rabbi Geiger—who eliminated ancient practices such as circumcision, separate seating for men and women, and *kashrut*—Rabbi Frankel opposed abandoning key Jewish rituals because they had been "hallowed by tradition." **What did he mean by that? How would Rabbi Geiger and Rabbi Hirsch have reacted to Frankel's defense of ancient rituals?** _____

Debate It

The split between religious traditionalists and modernists erupted in the mid-19th century, and the differences between them remain today. Traditionalists believe that God revealed every word of the Torah; therefore, it remains the touchstone of truth and the sole authority of behavior. For humans to imagine they can improve on it is mere folly. Modernists, on the other hand, believe that the Torah did not come into being at one time; instead, it records the spiritual and moral evolution of the Jewish people. Because Judaism continues to evolve and change, the laws of Torah must be adaptable.

Resolved: that although the source of the Torah is divinely inspired, its development lies in the judgment of humans.

Competing Values

עַם יִשְׂרָאֵל (*am yisrael*), The People of Israel — Just as Jacob wrestled with God's messenger and emerged with a new name, *Yisrael* (struggled with God), each generation after him will struggle with God, redefining the Covenant so that it remains eternally meaningful.

כִּתְבֵי קוֹדֶשׁ (*kitvei kodesh*), Canon of Sacred Texts — All societies elevate certain sacred texts to a level of supreme authority and rely on them as a guide to ethical living.

Reflections

Maimonides, the great Torah scholar of the Middle Ages, taught that "the gates of interpretation are not closed." (Guide to the Perplexed 2, 25).

How are you interpreting and redefining the Covenant?

How do you decide which Jewish beliefs and practices you adopt?

What do you think Judaism will look like 100 years from now?

Echoes from the Past
Rabba Sara Hurwitz (June 2009)

Rabbi Avi Weiss stood confidently before his congregation. The members had always supported his political activism and his confrontational style—even when he was arrested at Auschwitz for protesting the construction of a Catholic convent at that hallowed site. But the radical step he was about to take would outrage the Orthodox establishment like nothing else he had done. Nevertheless, Weiss proceeded.

"Sara," he said proudly, turning to the young woman. "We bless you as you rise and come forward to join me in officially becoming part of the religious leadership of Israel and officially becoming a full member of our clergy!" Cheers arose from the congregation.

Sara Hurwitz beamed. After eight years of intensive study, she had realized her dream to serve the Jewish community as a female Orthodox rabbi. The title that Weiss gave his prized student, however, was ambiguous. Though he recognized that the "authority of Torah will rest upon her shoulders," he avoided calling her rabbi. Instead, he identified her as *MaHaRaT*, a Hebrew acronym he invented that means a leader in Jewish law, spirituality, and Torah.

Some of Weiss' supporters objected to the term; they preferred *rabba*, the feminine form of rabbi.

Hurwitz gladly accepted the title. A month later, when she became dean of Yeshivat Maharat, the seminary Rabbi Weiss founded to train Orthodox women as legal and spiritual leaders, Hurwitz described the school's philosophy: "The time has come," she said, "for women to transform their knowledge into service…to stand together, with our male counterparts, as spiritual leaders of our community. And not only because women should have the same opportunities as men— although they should—and not only because women can learn and achieve on par with men—although they can. But because women, as Jewish leaders, have so many singular and unique gifts to offer, so much to contribute to the larger Jewish community."

After a year, Rabbi Weiss gave the title of rabba *to Sara Hurwitz, explaining, "This will make it clear to everyone that Sara Hurwitz is a full member of our rabbinic staff, a rabbi with the additional quality of a distinct woman's voice."*

1885	1897	
The Pittsburgh Platform of the Reform movement declares: *"We consider ourselves . . . a religious community, and therefore expect neither a return to Palestine . . . nor the restoration of the laws concerning the Jewish state."*	First Zionist Congress in Basel, Switzerland. Afterwards, Theodor Herzl writes in his diary: *"At Basel I founded the Jewish state. . . . Maybe in five years, certainly in fifty, everyone will realize it."*	Isaac M. Wise crafts a resolution that disapproves of *"the establishment of a Jewish State."* Moreover, Wise writes *"that the object of Judaism is not political nor national, but spiritual. . . ."*

A Jewish State?
The Debate Over Zionism

> "The Promised Land ... where at last we can live as free men on our own soil and die in peace in our own homeland.
>
> (Theodor Herzl)

> We are perfectly satisfied with our political and social position. It makes no difference to us... what particular spot of the earth's surface we occupy.
>
> (Rabbi Isaac M. Wise)

The crowd strained for a glimpse of the Jewish traitor, Captain Alfred Dreyfus, who had been convicted in 1894 of offering to sell French military secrets to the Germans. The only evidence against him was a shredded letter that a spy, posing as a cleaning lady, had pulled from a garbage can in the German embassy. After the letter was painstakingly reassembled, a graphologist testified that although the handwriting did not resemble Dreyfus' style, the letter was his obvious attempt to disguise his writing. On the basis of this flimsy evidence, Dreyfus was convicted.

In the courtyard of the École Militaire, Dreyfus struggled to remain dignified. Amid shouts of "death to Jews," an officer, called a degrader, stripped the condemned man's insignia and broke his sword. Dreyfus was paraded around the courtyard, where the crowd spat at him. Theodore Herzl, an assimilated Jewish journalist from Vienna, was watching this anti-Semitic spectacle. The hatred he witnessed led him to conclude that anti-Semitism was an eternal stain on society. By 1896, he had written *The Jewish State*, the Zionist manifesto that called for a national homeland for the Jewish people.

1898
At the Second Zionist Congress, Herzl initiated a campaign, called "Conquer the Communities," to convince Jewish leaders of Zionism's importance.

1901
Jewish National Fund was created at the Fifth Zionist Congress. Its purpose: raise funds for land purchase in Palestine.

1917
The Balfour Declaration declares that "*His Majesty's Government view*[s] *with favour the establishment in Palestine of a national home for the Jewish people....*"

Clarification

1 In his book *The Jewish State*, Herzl emphasized willpower, saying that Jews "who will it shall achieve their state." **What gave Herzl such confidence? Can you recount other examples of willpower overcoming great odds?** _____

_____

_____

2 Political Zionism proclaims that the Jews, like other nations, deserve a homeland. **Why did many American Jews disagree?** _____

_____

_____

_____

3 During the Dreyfus affair, certain French writers and politicians blamed France's problems on Jewish immigrants, even though many had lived in France for decades. These anti-Semites claimed that Jews brought alien values to Christian France. **How was America's response to Jewish immigration in the late 19th century different?** _____

_____

_____

4 To revitalize Jewish cultural and spiritual life, cultural Zionists denied the need for a political state; instead, they advocated small settlements in Palestine that would create a renaissance in Jewish culture. **How do you think American Jews reacted to cultural Zionism?** _____

_____

_____

_____

The Great Debate

Here is an imagined conversation between Herzl and Wise. Although there is no evidence that these men ever met, they were aware of each other's activities. This debate incorporates language from Herzl's diary and speeches, and from Wise's address to the Central Conference of American Rabbis.

Herzl: *The Jewish question still exists. It would be foolish to deny it. We have honestly striven everywhere to merge ourselves in the social life of surrounding communities, and to preserve only the faith of our fathers. It has not been permitted to us.*

Wise: *The persecution of the Jews in Russia and Romania and the anti-Semitic hatred against the Jewish race and religion, as it still exists in Germany, Austria, and partly in France roused among the persecuted and outraged persons the hapless feeling of being hated strangers among hostile Gentiles. [But here] we are perfectly satisfied with our political and social position.*

Herzl: *We are one people—One People! [We need] the Promised Land, where it is all right for us to have hooked noses, black or red beards, and bow legs without being despised for these things alone. Where at last we can live as free men on our own soil and die in peace in our homeland.*

Wise: *It makes no difference to us … what particular spot of the earth's surface we occupy. We want freedom, equality, justice and equity to reign and govern the community in which we live. All this agitation on the other side of the ocean concerns us very little.*

Herzl: *We are one people—our enemies have made us one without our consent, as repeatedly happens in history. Distress binds us together, and, thus united, we suddenly discover our strength. Yes, we are strong enough to form a state, and indeed, a model state.*

Wise: *[You] revive among certain classes of people the political national sentiment of olden times, and turn the mission of Israel from the province of religion and humanity to the narrow political and national field, where Judaism loses its universal and sanctified ground.*

Herzl: *Zionism is a return to the Jewish fold even before it becomes a return to the Jewish land.*

Wise: *[Zionism] is a momentary inebriation of morbid minds, and a prostitution of Israel's cause to a madman's dance....*

Herzl: *God would not have preserved our people for so long if we did not have another role to play in the history of mankind.*

Cross Examination

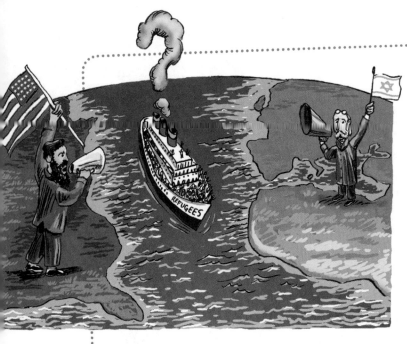

Herzl attributes Jewish solidarity to anti-Semitism. **Do you agree or disagree? Why?**

_____

Herzl argued that the only way to prevent anti-Semitism was to create a Jewish national homeland. **How has his idea fared during the 20th century?** _____

_____

Rabbi Wise considered Zionism "a prostitution of Israel's cause." **What did he mean? Do you agree with him?** _____

Rabbi Wise accused Herzl of turning the divine mission of Israel from religion and humanity to petty politics. **How has history proven him correct? Proven him wrong?** _____

_____

Debate It

Israel's Law of Return guarantees immediate citizenship to any Jew who returns to Israel. (Non-Jews must satisfy a host of conditions, including a residency requirement.) Determining who is a Jew, however, has pitted the Orthodox community against the liberal Jewish community and Israeli secular authorities. The Law of Return currently defines a Jew as someone who was born to a Jewish mother, or who converted to Judaism. Orthodox authorities have attempted repeatedly to change the law so that only Orthodox conversions would qualify. Liberal Jewish organizations argue that such a change would divide the Jewish community.

Resolved: that Israel, like the United States, should have a strict separation between religion and the state.

Competing Values

The dream of Jewish nationalism, לְאוּמָנוּת (l'umanut), was realized in 1948, when the State of Israel was established. An independent state provides an opportunity for Jews to express national identity in all areas of life, including legislative and judicial systems.

The term "Jewish religion," הֲדָת הַיַּהֲדוּת (hadat hayahadut), describes the beliefs, ritual behaviors, and religious laws of the Jewish people.

Reflections

Zionism is the Jewish national movement of rebirth and renewal in the Land of Israel — the historical birthplace of the Jewish people.

Describe an instance of anti-Semitism you personally experienced, or one you witnessed. **How did it affect your Jewish identity?**

Describe your feelings about the State of Israel. Describe your feelings about Israel, the homeland of the Jewish people. Explore the differences between the two feelings.

What does Zionism mean to you?

Case Study

(H.C. 230186)

Supreme Court of Israel, Jerusalem

Israel Supreme Court sitting as the High Court of Justice, in the matter between Shoshana (Susan) Miller, petitioner, versus the Minister of Interior

Susan Miller studied for conversion with a Reform rabbi. She read Jewish history, explored the meaning and practice of Jewish holidays, and learned to read Hebrew. She concluded her training with immersion in the ritual bath, and received a conversion certificate from the Reform movement.

In 1985, Miller moved to Israel. She applied for and was granted citizenship under the Law of Return. Like all new citizens, Miller applied for an identity card, which identifies a person's nationality and religion. To prove that she was Jewish, Miller presented her Reform conversion certificate, but the registrar told her that the case must be referred to the Rabbinical Court. Moreover, the official suggested that Miller register herself as a Christian, or that the religion status remain blank. Miller objected, and was ultimately told that the Ministry of Interior would register her as "Jewish (Converted)."

Miller applied to the High Court for an order to force officials to register her as Jewish without mentioning she was a convert.

Justice Menachem Elon agreed with the petitioner; namely, that officials had no authority to add the word "converted" to the document. Elon argued that doing so violated Jewish law. He cited the following passage from a 1984 precedent of the Supreme Court: "The Jewish People does not 'seek souls' to attract members of other peoples to its ranks (Micah 4:5; Maimonides, Melachim 8:10); but once the son of another people has joined the Jewish People, he becomes a member of that people, both as to his rights and obligations."

The petition was allowed on December 2, 1986.

Online Resources

Log on to www.behrmanhouse.com/greatdebates for additional information that will maximize the benefits of this book, including:

- character profiles of the historic debaters featured in each chapter

- insights into Jewish values

- instructions on how to organize a Lincoln-Douglas values conflict debate

- tips on building an effective argument

- topic analysis on each resolution